The Dhamma Theory

PHILOSOPHICAL CORNERSTONE OF THE ABHIDHAMMA

Y. Karunadasa

Buddhist Publication Society

Kandy • Sri Lanka

Published in 1996

Buddhist Publication Society
P.O. Box 61
54, Sangharaja Mawatha
Kandy, Sri Lanka

ISBN 955-24-0137-2

An earlier version of this paper was published by the Shin Buddhist Comprehensive Research Institute, Annual Memoirs.

Typeset at the BPS

Printed in Sri Lanka by
Karunaratne & Sons Ltd.
647, Kularatne Mawatha
Colombo 10

THE WHEEL PUBLICATION NO. 412/413

CONTENTS

Introduction 1

I. The Early Version of the *Dhamma* Theory 3

II. The Development of the Theory 10

III. *Paññatti* and the Two Truths 27

Notes 41

Abbreviations 48

INTRODUCTION

During the first two centuries following the Buddha's parinibbāna there took place, within the early Buddhist community, a move towards a comprehensive and precise systematization of the teachings disclosed by the Master in his discourses. The philosophical systems that emerged from this refined analytical approach to the doctrine are collectively called the Abhidhamma. Both the Theravāda and the Sarvāstivāda, the two major conservative schools in the early Sangha, had their own Abhidhammas, each based on a distinct Abhidhamma Piṭaka. It is likely too that other schools had also developed philosophical systems along similar lines, though records of them did not survive the passage of time.

All the different modes of analysis and classification found in the Abhidhamma stem from a single philosophical principle, which gave direction and shape to the entire project of systematization. This principle is the notion that all the phenomena of empirical existence are made up of a number of elementary constituents, the ultimate realities behind the manifest phenomena. These elementary constituents, the building blocks of experience, are called *dhammas*.[1] The *dhamma* theory is not merely one principle among others in the body of Abhidhamma philosophy but the base upon which the entire system rests. It would thus be quite fitting to call this theory the cornerstone of the Abhidhamma. But the *dhamma* theory was intended from the start to be more than a mere hypothetical scheme. It arose from the need to make sense out of experiences in meditation and was designed as a guide for meditative contemplation and insight. The Buddha had taught that to see the world correctly is to see—not persons and substances—but bare phenomena (*suddhadhammā*) arising and perishing in accordance with their conditions. The task the Abhidhamma specialists set themselves was to specify exactly what these "bare phenomena" are and to show how they relate to other "bare phenomena" to make up our "common sense" picture of the world.

The *dhamma* theory was not peculiar to any one school of Buddhism but penetrated all the early schools, stimulating the growth of their different versions of the Abhidhamma. The Sarvāstivāda version of the theory, together with its critique by the Mādhyamikas, has been critically studied by a number of modern scholars. The Theravāda version, however, has received less attention. There are sound reasons for believing that the Pāli Abhidhamma Piṭaka contains one of the earliest forms of the *dhamma* theory, perhaps even the oldest version. This theory did not remain static but evolved over the centuries as Buddhist thinkers sought to draw out the implications of the theory and to respond to problems it posed for the critical intellect. Thus the *dhamma* theory was repeatedly enriched, first by the Abhidhamma commentaries and then by the later exegetical literature and the medieval compendia of Abhidhamma, the so-called "little finger manuals" such as the *Abhidhammattha-saṅgaha*, which in turn gave rise to their own commentaries.

In the present paper I will attempt to trace the main stages in the origin and development of the *dhamma* theory and to explore its philosophical implications. Part I will discuss the early version of the theory as represented by the Abhidhamma Piṭaka. At this stage the theory was not yet precisely articulated but remained in the background as the unspoken premise of Abhidhamma analysis. It was during the commentarial period that an attempt was made to work out the implications of early Abhidhamma thought, and it is this development that I will treat in Part II. Finally, in Part III, I will discuss two other topics that received philosophical study as a consequence of the *dhamma* theory, namely, the category of the nominal and the conceptual (*paññatti*) and the theory of the twofold truth. Both of these were considered necessary measures to preserve the validity of the *dhamma* theory in relation to our routine, everyday understanding of ourselves and the world in which we dwell.

I. THE EARLY VERSION OF THE DHAMMA THEORY

Although the *dhamma* theory is an Abhidhammic innovation, the antecedent trends that led to its formulation and its basic ingredients can be traced to the early Buddhist scriptures which seek to analyse empiric individuality and its relation to the external world. In the discourses of the Buddha there are five such modes of analysis. The first, the analysis into *nāma* and *rūpa*,[2] is the most elementary in the sense that it specifies the two main components, the mental and the corporeal aspects, of the empiric individual. The second is that into the five *khandhas* (aggregates): corporeality (*rūpa*), sensation (*vedanā*), perception (*saññā*), mental formations (*saṅkhārā*), and consciousness (*viññāṇa*).[3] The third is that into six *dhātus* (elements): earth (*paṭhavī*), water (*āpo*), temperature (*tejo*), air (*vāyo*), space (*ākāsa*), and consciousness (*viññāṇa*).[4] The fourth is that into twelve *āyatanas* (avenues of sense-perception and mental cognition): the eye, ear, nose, tongue, body, and mind; and their corresponding objects: visible form, sound, smell, taste, touch, and mental objects.[5] The fifth is that into eighteen *dhātus* (elements), an elaboration of the immediately preceding mode obtained by the addition of the six kinds of consciousness which arise from the contact between the sense organs and their objects. The six additional items are the visual, auditory, olfactory, gustatory, tactile, and mental consciousnesses.[6]

Now the purposes for which Buddhism resorts to these analyses are varied. For instance, the main purpose of the *khandha*-analysis is to show that there is no ego either inside or outside the five *khandhas* which go to make up the so-called empiric individuality. None of the *khandhas* belongs to me (*n'etaṁ mama*), they do not correspond to "I" (*n'eso'ham asmi*), nor are they my self (*n'eso me attā*).[7] Thus the main purpose of this analysis is to prevent the intrusion of the notions of "mine," "I," and "my self" into what is otherwise an impersonal and egoless congeries of mental and physical phenomena. On the other hand, the analysis into eighteen *dhātus* is often resorted to in order to show that consciousness is neither a soul nor an extension of a soul-substance but a mental phenomenon which comes into being as a result of certain conditions: there is no independent consciousness which exists in its own right.[8] In similar fashion each analysis is used to explain certain features of sentient existence. It is, in fact, with reference to these five kinds of analysis that Buddhism frames its fundamental doctrines. The very fact that there are at least five kinds of analysis shows that none of them can be taken as final or absolute. Each represents the world of experience in its totality, yet represents it from a pragmatic standpoint determined by the particular doctrine which it is intended to illuminate.

The Abhidhammic doctrine of *dhammas* developed from an

attempt to draw out the full implications of these five types of analysis. It will be seen that if each analysis is examined in relation to the other four, it is found to be further analysable. That the first, the analysis into *nāma* and *rūpa*, is further analysable is seen by the second, the analysis into the five *khandhas*. For in the second, the *nāma*-component of the first is analysed into sensation, perceptions, mental formations, and consciousness. That the analysis into *khandhas*, too, can be further analysed is shown not only by the use of the term *khandha*, which means "group," but also by the next analysis, that into six *dhātus*. For in the latter, the *rūpa*-component of the former is analysed into four, namely, earth water, temperature, and air. That the analysis into six *dhātus* is also further analysable is seen from the fact that consciousness, which is reckoned here as one item, is made into four in the *khandha*-analysis. That the same situation is true of the analysis into twelve *āyatanas* is shown by the next analysis, that into eighteen *dhātus,* because the latter is an elaboration of the former. This leaves us with the last, the *dhātu*-analysis with eighteen items. Can this be considered final? This supposition too must be rejected, because although consciousness is here itemized as sixfold, its invariable concomitants such as sensation (*vedanā*) and perception (*saññā*) are not separately mentioned. It will thus be seen that none of the five analyses can be considered exhaustive. In each case one or more items is further analysable.

This, it seems to me, is the line of thought that led the Ābhidhammikas to evolve still another mode of analysis which in their view is not amenable to further analysis. This new development, which is more or less common to all the systems of Abhidhamma, is the analysis of the world of experience into what came to be known as *dharmas* (Skt) or *dhammas* (Pāli).

The term *dhamma*, of course, looms large in the discourses of the Buddha, found in a variety of senses which have to be determined by the specific context. In the Abhidhamma, however, the term assumes a more technical meaning, referring to those items that result when the process of analysis is taken to its ultimate limits. In the Theravāda Abhidhamma, for instance, the aggregate of corporeality (of the *khandha*-analysis) is broken down into twenty-eight items called *rūpa-dhammas*. The next three aggregates—sensation, perception, and mental formations—are together arranged into fifty-two items called *cetasikas*. The fifth, consciousness, is counted as one item with eighty-nine varieties and is referred to as *citta*.[9]

Thus the *dhamma*-analysis is an addition to the previous five modes of analyses. Its scope is the same, the world of conscious experience, but its divisions are finer and more exhaustive. This situation in itself does not constitute a radical departure from the earlier tradition, for it does not as yet involve a view of existence that is at variance with that of early Buddhism. There is, however, this situation to be noted: Since the analysis into *dhammas* is the most exhaustive, the previous five modes of analysis become subsumed under it as five subordinate classifications.

The definition and classification of these *dhammas* and the explanation of their inter-connections form the main subject matter of the canonical Abhidhamma. The Ābhidhammikas presuppose that to understand any given item properly is to know it in all its relations, under all aspects recognized in the doctrinal and practical discipline of Buddhism. Therefore, in the Abhidhamma Piṭaka, they have classified the same material in different ways and from different points of view. This explains why, in the *Dhammasaṅgaṇī* and other Abhidhamma treatises, one encounters innumerable lists of classifications. Although such lists may appear repetitive, even monotonous, they serve a useful purpose, bringing into relief, not only the individual characteristic of each *dhamma*, but also its relations to other *dhammas*.

With this same aim in view, in bringing out the nature of the *dhammas*, the Abhidhamma resorts to two complementary methods: that of analysis (*bheda*) and that of synthesis (*saṅgaha*). The analytical method dominates in the *Dhammasaṅgaṇī*, which according to tradition is the first book of the Abhidhamma Piṭaka; for here we find a complete catalogue of the *dhammas*, each with a laconic definition. The synthetical method is more characteristic of the *Paṭṭhāna*, the last book of the Abhidhamma Piṭaka; for here we find an exhaustive catalogue of the conditional relations of the *dhammas*. The combined use of these two methods shows that, according to the methodological apparatus employed in the Abhidhamma, "a complete description of a thing requires, besides its analysis, also a statement of its relations to certain other things."[10] Thus if analysis plays an important role in the Abhidhamma's methodology, no less important a role is played by synthesis. Analysis shows that the world of experience is resolvable into a plurality of factors; synthesis shows that these factors are not discrete entities existing in themselves but inter-connected and inter-dependent nodes in a complex web of relationships. It is only for the purpose of definition and description that things are artificially dissected. In actuality the world given to experience is a vast network of tightly interwoven relations.

This fact needs emphasis because the Abhidhammic doctrine of *dhammas* has sometimes been represented as a radical pluralism. Such an interpretation is certainly not admissible. It is mostly Stcherbatsky's writings,[11] mainly based on the Sarvāstivāda sources, that has given currency to this incorrect interpretation. "Up to the present time," observes Nyanaponika Thera, "it has been a regular occurrence in the history of physics, metaphysics, and psychology that when a whole has been successfully dissolved by analysis, the resultant parts come again to be regarded as little Wholes."[12] This is the kind of process that culminates in radical pluralism. As we shall soon see, about a hundred years after the formulation of the *dhamma*-theory, such a trend surfaced within certain schools of Buddhist thought and culminated in the view that the *dhammas* exist in all three periods of time. But the Pāli Abhidhamma Piṭaka did not succumb to this error of conceiving the *dhammas* as ultimate unities or discrete entities. In the Pāli tradition it is only for the sake of definition and description that each *dhamma* is postulated as if it were a separate entity; but in reality it is by no means a solitary phenomenon having an existence of its own. This is precisely why the mental and material *dhammas* are often presented in inter-connected groups. In presenting them thus the danger inherent in narrowly analytical methods has been avoided—the danger, namely, of elevating the factors resulting from analysis to the status of genuinely separate entities. Thus if analysis shows that composite things cannot be considered as ultimate unities, synthesis shows that the factors into which the apparently composite things are analysed (*ghana-vinibbhoga*) are not discrete entities.[13]

If this Abhidhammic view of existence, as seen from its doctrine of *dhammas*, cannot be interpreted as a radical pluralism, neither can it be interpreted as an out-and-out monism. For what are called *dhammas*—the component factors of the universe, both within us and outside us—are not fractions of an absolute unity but a multiplicity of co-ordinate factors. They are not reducible to, nor do they emerge from, a single reality, the fundamental postulate of monistic metaphysics. If they are to be interpreted as phenomena, this should be done with the proviso that they are phenomena with no corresponding noumena, no hidden underlying ground. For they are not manifestations of some mysterious metaphysical substratum, but processes taking place due to the interplay of a multitude of conditions.

In thus evolving a view of existence which cannot be interpreted in either monistic or pluralistic terms, the Abhidhamma accords with the "middle doctrine" of early Buddhism. This doctrine avoids both the eternalist view of existence which maintains that everything exists absolutely (*sabbaṁ atthi*)[14] and the opposite nihilistic view which maintains that absolutely nothing exists (*sabbaṁ natthi*).[15] It also avoids, on the one hand, the monistic view that everything is reducible to a common ground, some sort of self-substance (*sabbaṁ ekattaṁ*)[16] and, on the other, the opposite pluralistic view that the whole of existence is resolvable into a concatenation of discrete entities (*sabbaṁ puthuttaṁ*).[17] Transcending these two pairs of extremist views, the middle doctrine explains that phenomena arise in dependence on other phenomena without a self-subsisting noumenon which serves as the ground of their being.

The inter-connection and inter-dependence of these *dhammas* are not explained on the basis of the dichotomy between substance and quality. Consequently, a given *dhamma* does not inhere in another as its quality, nor does it serve another as its substance. The so-called substance is only a product of our imagination. The distinction between substance and quality is denied because such a distinction leaves the door open for the intrusion of the doctrine of a substantial self (*attavāda*) with all that it entails. Hence it is with reference to causes and conditions that the inter-connection of the *dhammas* should be understood. The conditions are not different from the *dhammas*, for it is the *dhammas* themselves that constitute the conditions. How each *dhamma* serves as a condition (*paccaya*) for the origination of another (*paccayuppanna*) is explained on the basis of the system of conditioned genesis (*paccayākāra-naya*).[18] This system, which consists of twenty-four conditions, aims at demonstrating the inter-dependence and dependent co-origination (*paṭicca-samuppāda*) of all *dhammas* in respect of both their temporal sequence and their spatial concomitance.

II. The Development of the Theory

The foregoing is a brief summary of the earliest phase of the *dhamma* theory as presented in the books of the Pāli Abhidhamma Piṭaka, particularly the *Dhammasaṅgaṇī* and the *Paṭṭhāna*. About a hundred years after its formulation, as a reaction against it, there emerged what came to be known as *puggalavāda* or "personalism,"[19] a philosophical theory that led to a further clarification of the nature of *dhammas*. Now here it may be noted that according to the early Buddhist discourses there is no denial as such of the concept of the person (*puggala*), if by "person" is understood, not an enduring entity distinct from the five *khandhas* nor an agent within the *khandhas*, but simply the sum total of the five causally connected and ever-changing *khandhas*. From the point of view of the *dhamma*-analysis, this can be restated by substituting the term *dhamma* for the term *khandha*, for the *dhammas* are the factors that obtain by analysis of the *khandhas*.

However, this way of defining the concept of person (*puggala*) did not satisfy some Buddhists. In their opinion the *dhamma* theory as presented by the Theravādins led to a complete depersonalization of the individual being and consequently failed to provide adequate explanations of such concepts as rebirth and moral responsibility. Hence these thinkers insisted on positing the person (*puggala*) as an additional reality distinct from the *khandhas* or *dhammas*. As recorded in the *Kathāvatthu*, the "Points of Controversy," the main contention of the Puggalavādins or "Personalists" is that the person is known in a real and ultimate sense (*saccikaṭṭhaparamaṭṭhena upalabbhati*).[20] Against this proposition a number of counter-arguments are adduced, which need not concern us here. What interests us, however, is that in denying that the person is known in a real and ultimate sense, the Theravādins admit that the *khandhas* or *dhammas* are known in a real and ultimate sense. Thus in their view what is real and ultimate is not the person but the *khandhas* or *dhammas* that enter into its composition.[21]

Now the use of the two words, *saccikaṭṭha* and *paramaṭṭha* ("real and ultimate") as indicative of the nature of *dhammas* seems to give the impression that in denying the reality of the person the Theravādins have overstressed the reality of the *dhammas*. Does this amount to the admission that the *dhammas* are real and discrete entities existing in their own right? Such a conclusion, it appears to us, is not tenable. For if the *dhammas* are defined as real and ultimate, this means, not that they partake of the nature of absolute entities, but that they are not further reducible to any other reality, to some kind of substance which underlies them. That is to say, there is no "behind the scenes" substance from which they emerge and to which they finally return. This means, in effect, that the *dhammas* represent the final limits of the Abhidhammic analysis of empirical existence.

Hence this new definition does not erode the empirical foundation of the *dhamma* theory as presented by the Theravādins. Moreover, this view is quite consonant with the statement occurring in the earlier texts that the *dhammas* come to be without having been (*ahutvā sambhonti*) and disappear without any residue (*hutvā paṭiventi*).[22]

Why, unlike the *dhammas,* the person (*puggala*) is not recognized as real and ultimate needs explanation. Since the person is the sum total of the causally connected mental and corporeal *dhammas* that constitute the empiric individual, it lends itself to further analysis. And what is subject to analysis cannot be an irreducible datum of cognition. The opposite situation is true of the *dhammas*. This brings into focus two levels of reality: that which is amenable to analysis and that which defies further analysis. Analysability is the mark of composite things, and non-analysability the mark of the elementary constituents, the *dhammas*.

Another doctrinal controversy that has left its mark on the Theravāda version of the *dhamma* theory is the one concerning the theory of tri-temporal existence (*sarvamastivāda*). What is revolutionary about this theory, advanced by the Sarvāstivādins, is that it introduced a metaphysical dimension to the doctrine of *dhammas* and thus paved the way for the erosion of its empirical foundation. For this theory makes an empirically unverifiable distinction between the actual being of the *dhammas* as phenomena and their ideal being as noumena. It assumes that the substances of all *dhammas* persist in all the three divisions of time—past, present, and future—while their manifestations as phenomena are impermanent and subject to change. Accordingly, a *dhamma* actualizes itself only in the present moment of time, but "in essence" it continues to subsist in all the three temporal periods. As is well known, this resulted in the transformation of the *dhamma* theory into a *svabhāvavāda*, "the doctrine of own-nature." It also paved the way for a veiled recognition, if not for a categorical assumption, of the distinction between substance and quality. What interests us here is the fact that although the Theravādins rejected this metaphysical theory of tri-temporal existence, including its qualified version as accepted by the Kāśyapīyas,[23] it was not without its influence on the Theravāda version of the *dhamma* theory.

This influence is to be seen in the post-canonical exegetical literature of Sri Lanka where, for the first time, the term *sabhāva* (Skt *svabhāva*) came to be used as a synonym for *dhamma*. Hence the recurrent definition: "*Dhammas* are so called because they bear their own nature" (*attano sabhāvaṁ dhārentī ti dhammā*).[24] Now the question that arises here is whether the Theravādins used the term *sabhāva* in the same sense as the Sarvāstivādins did. Did the Theravādins assume the metaphysical view that the substance of a *dhamma* persists throughout the three phases of time? In other words, does this amount to the admission that there is a duality between the *dhamma* and its *sabhāva*, between the bearer and the borne, a dichotomy which goes against the grain of the Buddhist doctrine of *anattā*?

This situation has to be considered in the context of the logical apparatus used by the Ābhidhammikas in defining the *dhammas*. This involves three main kinds of definition. The first is called agency definition (*kattu-sādhana*) because it attributes agency to the thing to be defined. Such, for example, is the definition of *citta* (consciousness) as "that which thinks" (*cintetī ti cittaṁ*).[25] The second is called instrumental definition (*karaṇa-sādhana*) because it attributes instrumentality to the thing to be defined. Such, for example, is the definition of *citta* as "that through which one thinks" (*cinteti ti etena cittaṁ*).[26] The third is called definition by nature (*bhāva-sādhana*) whereby the abstract nature of the thing to be defined is brought into focus. Such, for example, is the definition,"The mere act of thinking itself is *citta* (*cintanamattam eva cittaṁ*)." [27]

The first two kinds of definition, it is maintained, are provisional and as such are not valid from an ultimate point of view.[28] This is because the attribution of agency and instrumentality invests a *dhamma* with a duality when it is actually a unitary and unique phenomenon. Such attribution also leads to the wrong assumption that a given *dhamma* is a substance with inherent qualities or an agent which performs some kind of action. Such definitions are said to be based on tentative attribution (*samāropana*)[29] and thus are not ultimately valid.[30] It is as a matter of convention (*vohāra*), and for the sole purpose of facilitating the grasp of the idea to be conveyed,[31] that a duality is assumed by the mind in defining the *dhamma*, which is actually devoid of such duality.[32] Thus both agency and instrumental definitions are resorted to for the convenience of description, and as such they are not to be understood in their direct literal sense. On the other hand, what is called definition by nature (*bhāvasādhana*) is the one that is admissible in an ultimate sense.[33] This is because this type of definition brings into focus the real nature of a given *dhamma* without attributing agency or instrumentality to it, an attribution which creates the false notion that there is a duality within a unitary *dhamma*.

It is in the context of these implications that the definition of *dhamma* as that which bears its own nature has to be understood. Clearly, this is a definition according to agency (*kattu-sādhana*), and hence its validity is provisional. From this definition, therefore, one cannot conclude that a given *dhamma* is a substantial bearer of its qualities or "own-nature." The duality between *dhamma* and *sabhāva* is only an attribution made for the convenience of definition. For in actual fact both terms denote the same actuality. Hence it is categorically stated that apart from *sabhāva* there is no distinct entity called a *dhamma*,[34] and that the term *sabhāva* signifies the mere fact of being a *dhamma*.[35]

If the *dhamma* has no function distinct from its *sabhāva*,[36] and if *dhamma* and *sabhāva* denote the same thing,[37] why is the *dhamma* invested with the function of bearing its own-nature? For this implies the recognition of an agency distinct from the *dhamma*. This, it is observed, is done not only to conform with the inclinations of those who are to be instructed,[38] but also to impress upon us the fact that there is no agent behind the *dhamma*.[39] The point being emphasized is that the dynamic world of sensory experience is not due to causes other than the selfsame *dhammas* into which it is finally reduced. It is the interconnection of the *dhammas* through causal relations that explains the variety and diversity of contingent existence and not some kind of transempirical reality which serves as their metaphysical ground. Nor is it due to the fiat of a Creator God[40] because there is no Divine Creator over and above the flow of mental and material phenomena.[41]

Stated otherwise, the definition of *dhamma* as that which bears its own-nature means that any *dhamma* represents a distinct fact of empirical existence which is not shared by other *dhammas*. Hence *sabhāva* is also defined as that which is not held in common by others (*anaññasādhāraṇa*),[42] as the nature peculiar to each *dhamma* (*āveṇika-sabhāva*),[43] and as the own-nature is not predicable of other *dhammas* (*asādhāraṇa-sabhāva*).[44] It is also observed that if the *dhammas* are said to have own-nature (*sakabhāva* = *sabhāva*), this is only a tentative device to drive home the point that there is no other-nature (*para-bhāva*) from which they emerge and to which they finally lapse.[45]

Now this commentarial definition of *dhamma* as *sabhāva* poses an important problem, for it seems to go against an earlier Theravāda tradition recorded in the *Paṭisambhidāmagga*. This canonical text specifically states that the five aggregates are devoid of own-nature (*sabhāvena-suññaṁ*).[46] Since the *dhammas* are the elementary constituents of the five aggregates, this should mean that the *dhammas*, too, are devoid of own-nature. What is more, does not the very use of the term *sabhāva*, despite all the qualifications under which it is used, give the impression that a given *dhamma* exists in its own right? And does this not amount to the admission that a *dhamma* is some kind of substance?

The commentators were not unaware of these implications and they therefore took the necessary steps to forestall such a conclusion. This they sought to do by supplementing the former definition with another which actually nullifies the conclusion that the *dhammas* might be quasi-substances. This additional definition states that a *dhamma* is not that which bears its own-nature, but that which is borne by its own conditions (*paccayehi dhāriyantī ti dhammā*).[47] Whereas the earlier definition is agent-denotation (*kattusādhana*) because it attributes an active role to the *dhamma*, elevating it to the position of an agent, the new definition is object-denotation (*kamma-sādhana*) because it attributes a passive role to the *dhamma* and thereby downgrades it to the position of an object. What is radical about this new definition is that it reverses the whole process which otherwise might culminate in the conception of *dhammas* as substances or bearers of their own-nature. What it seeks to show is that, far from being a bearer, a *dhamma* is being *borne* by its own conditions.

Consonant with this situation, it is also maintained that there is no other thing called a *dhamma* than the "quality" of being borne by conditions.[48] The same idea is expressed in the oft-recurrent statement that what is called a *dhamma* is the mere fact of occurrence due to appropriate conditions.[49] In point of fact, in commenting upon the *Paṭisambhidāmagga* statement that the five aggregates—and, by implication, the *dhammas*—are devoid of *sabhāva*, the commentator observes that since the aggregates have no self-nature, they are devoid of own-nature.[50] It will thus be seen that although the term *sabhāva* is used as a synonym for *dhamma*, it is interpreted in such a way that it means the very absence of *sabhāva* in any sense that implies a substantial mode of being.

Another common definition of *dhamma* is that which bears its own characteristic, *salakkhaṇa*.[51] Since *salakkhaṇa* is used in the same sense as *sabhāva*, this definition carries more or less the same implications. That each *dhamma* has its own characteristic is illustrated with reference to colour, which is one of the secondary material elements. Although colour is divisible as blue, yellow, etc., the characteristic peculiar to all varieties of colour is their visibility (*sanidassanatā*).[52] Hence it is also called *paccatta-lakkhaṇa*, individual characteristic.[53] As in the case of *dhamma* and *sabhāva*, so in the case of *dhamma* and *salakkhaṇa*, too, their duality is only a convenient assumption made for the purpose of definition. For it is a case of attributing duality to that which has no duality.[54] And since it is only an attribution it is based on interpretation (*kappanāsiddha*)[55] and not on actuality (*bhāvasiddha*).[56] Hence the definition of earth element (*paṭhavī-dhātu*) as "that which has" the characteristic of solidity (*kakkhaḷatta-lakkhaṇā*)[57] is said to be invalid from an ultimate point of view, because of the assumed duality between the earth element and its characteristic. The correct definition is the one which states that solidity itself is the earth element, for this does not assume a distinction between the characteristic and what is characterized thereby.[58]

As the own-characteristic (*salakkhaṇa*) represents the characteristic peculiar to each *dhamma*, the universal characteristics (*sāmañña-lakkhaṇa*) are the characteristics common to all the *dhammas*. If the former is individually predicable, the latter are universally predicable.[59] Their difference goes still further. As the own-characteristic is another name for the *dhamma*, it represents a fact having an objective counterpart. It is not a product of mental construction (*kappanā*)[60] but an actual datum of objective existence and as such an ultimate datum of sense experience. On the other hand, what is called universal characteristic has no objective existence because it is a product of mental construction, the synthetic function of mind, and is superimposed on the ultimate data of empirical existence.

On this interpretation, the three characteristics of conditioned reality (*saṅkhata-lakkhaṇa*)—namely, origination (*uppāda*), cessation (*vaya*), and the alteration of that which exists (*ṭhitassa aññathatta*)—are universal characteristics (*sāmañña-lakkhaṇa*). Because they have no objective reality they are not elevated to the status of *dhammas*. If they were to be so elevated, that would undermine the very foundation of the *dhamma* theory. If, for instance, origination (*uppāda*), subsistence (*ṭhiti*), and dissolution (*bhaṅga*)[61] are postulated as real and discrete entities, then it would be necessary to postulate another set of secondary characteristics to account for their own origination, subsistence, and dissolution, thus resulting in an infinite regress (*anavaṭṭhāna*).[62] This is the significance of the commentarial observation: "It is not correct to assume that origination originates, decay decays, and cessation ceases because such an assumption leads to the fallacy of infinite regress."[63] The difference between the particular characteristic and the universal characteristic is also shown in the way they become knowable (*ñeyya*), for while the particular characteristic is known as a datum of sense perception (*paccakkha-ñāṇa*), the universal characteristic is known through a process of inference (*anumāna-ñāṇa*).[64]

In what sense the *dhammas* represent the final limits into which empirical existence can be analysed is another question that drew the attention of the Theravāda commentators. It is in answer to this that the term *paramattha* came to be used as another expression for *dhamma*. It was noted earlier that the use of this term in this sense was occasioned by the Theravādins' response to the Puggalavādins' assertion that the person exists as real and ultimate. In the Abhidhammic exegesis this term *paramattha* is defined to mean that which has reached its highest (*uttama*),[65] implying thereby that the *dhammas* are ultimate existents with no possibility of further reduction. Hence own-nature (*sabhāva*) came to be further defined as ultimate nature (*paramattha-sabhāva*).[66]

The term *paramattha* is sometimes paraphased as *bhūtattha* (the actual).[67] This is explained to mean that the *dhammas* are not non-existent like an illusion or mirage or like the soul (*purisa*) and primordial nature (*pakati*) of the non-Buddhist schools of thought.[68] The evidence for their existence is not based either on conventions (*sammuti*) or on mere scriptural authority (*anussava*).[69] On the contrary, their very existence is vouchsafed by their own intrinsic nature.[70] The very fact of their existence is the very mark of their reality. As the *Visuddhimagga* observes: "It (= *dhamma*) is that which, for those who examine it with the eye of understanding, is not misleading like an illusion, deceptive like a mirage, or undiscoverable like the self of the sectarians, but is rather the domain of noble knowledge as the real unmisleading actual state."[71] The kind of existence implied here is not past or future existence, but present actual and verifiable existence (*saṁvijjamānatā*).[72] This emphasis on their actuality in the present phase of time rules out any association with the Sarvāstivādins' theory of tri-temporal existence. Thus, for the Theravādin, the use of the term *paramattha* does not carry any substantialist implications. It only means that the mental and material *dhammas* represent the utmost limits to which the analysis of empirical existence can be pushed.

The description of *dhammas* as *paramattha* means not only their objective existence (*paramatthato vijjamānatā*) but also their cognizability in an ultimate sense (*paramatthato upalabbhamānatā*).[73] The first refers to the fact that the *dhammas* obtain as the ultimate, irreducible data of empirical existence. The second refers to the fact that, as such, the content of our cognition can also be finally analysed into the self-same elements. This is not to suggest that it is only the *dhammas* that become objects of knowledge; for it is specifically stated that even *paññattis*, i.e. concepts, which are the products of the synthetical function of the mind and hence lack objective counterparts, are also knowable (*ñeyya*).[74]

In point of fact, in the technical terminology of the Abhidhamma, the term *dhamma* is sometimes used in a wider sense to include anything that is knowable.[75] In this sense, not only the ultimate realities—the *dhammas* proper—but also the products of mental interpretation are called *dhammas*. To distinguish the two, the latter are called *asabhāva-dhammas*, i.e. *dhammas* devoid of objective reality.[76] The use of this term in this wider sense is reminiscent of its earlier meaning as shown in the Pāli Nikāyas, where it is used in a very general sense to include all cognizable things on the empirical level. However, there is this situation to be noted: Although both *dhammas* and concepts (*paññattis* or *asabhāva-dhammas*) constitute the content of knowledge, it is into the *dhammas* that the content of knowledge can be finally analysed. Thus there is a close parallelism between the *dhammas* on the one hand and the contents of knowledge on the other. That is to say, the ultimate irreducible data of cognition are the subjective counterparts of the ultimate irreducible data of objective existence.

If the term *paramattha* brings into focus the irreducibility of the *dhammas*, the term *aviparītabhāva* shows their irreversibility.[77] This term means that the essential characteristic of a *dhamma* is non-alterable and non-transferable to any other *dhamma*.[78] It also means that it is impossible for a given *dhamma* to undergo any modification of its specific characteristic even when it is in association with some other *dhamma*.[79] The same situation remains true despite the differences in the time factor, for there is no modification in the nature of a *dhamma* corresponding to the divisions in time.[80] Since a *dhamma* and its intrinsic nature are the same (for the duality is only posited for purposes of explanation), to claim that its intrinsic nature undergoes modification is to deny its very existence.

The relative position of the *dhammas* is another aspect of the subject that requires clarification. Do they harmoniously blend into a unity or do they divide themselves into a plurality? In this connection we may do well to examine two of their important characteristics. One is their actual inseparability (*saṁsaṭṭhatā*, *avinibbhogatā*),[81] the other their conditioned origination (*sappaccayatā*).[82]

The first refers to the fact that in a given instance of mind or matter, the elementary constituents (= *dhammas*) that enter into its composition are not actually separable one from another. They exist in a state of inseparable association forming, so to say, a homogeneous unity. This idea is in consonance with an earlier tradition recorded in the early Buddhist discourses. For example, in the Mahāvedalla Sutta of the Majjhima Nikāya it is said that the three mental factors—sensation (*vedanā*), perception (*saññā*), and consciousness (*viññāṇa*)—are blended (*saṁsaṭṭha*) so harmoniously that it is impossible to separate them from one another and thus establish their identity.[83] The same idea finds expression in the *Milindapañha*.[84] When Nāgasena Thera is asked by King Milinda whether it is possible, in the case of mental factors which exist in harmonious combination (*ekato bhāvagata*), to separate them out and establish a plurality as: "This is contact, and this sensation, and this mentation, and this perception," and so on, the elder answers with a simile:

> "Suppose, O king, the cook in the royal household were to make a syrup or a sauce and were to put into it curds, and salt, and ginger, and cumin seed, and pepper and other ingredients. And suppose the king were to say to him: 'Pick out for me the flavours of the curds and of the salt, and of the ginger, and of the cumin seed, and of the pepper, and of all the things you have put into it.' Now would it be possible, great king, separating off one from another those flavours that had thus run together, to pick out each one, so that one could say: 'Here is the sourness, and here the saltiness, and here the pungency, and here the acidity, and here the astringency, and here the sweetness'?"[85]

In like manner, it is maintained, we should understand the position of the mental *dhammas* in relation to one another.[86]

This situation is true of the material *dhammas*, too. In this connection the *Atthasālinī* adds that the material *dhammas*, such as colour, taste, odour, etc., cannot be separated from one another like particles of sand.[87] The colour of the mango, for instance, cannot be physically separated from its taste or odour. They remain in inseparable association. This is what is called positional inseparability (*padesato avinibbhogatā*).[88] On the basis of this principle of positional inseparability it is maintained that there is no quantitative difference (*pamāṇato*) among the material elements that enter into the composition of material objects. The difference is only qualitative. And this qualitative difference is based on what is called *ussada*, i.e. intensity or extrusion.[89] To give an example: As the four primary elements of matter are invariably present in every instance of matter, for they are necessarily co-existent (*sahajāta*) and positionally inseparable (*padesato avinibbhoga*),[90] the question arises why there is a diversity in material objects. The diversity, it is maintained, is not due to a difference in quantity (*pamāṇa*) but to a difference in intensity (*ussada*).[91] That is to say, in a given material object one primary element is more intense than the others. For instance, in a relatively solid thing such as a stone, although all the primary elements are present, the earth element is more intense or "extruded" than the others. So is the water element in liquids, the heat element in fire, and the air element in gases.[92]

The best illustration for the relative position of the material elements is given in the *Visuddhimagga* where it is said: "And just as whomsoever the great creatures such as the spirits grasp hold of (possess), they have no standing place either inside him or outside him and yet they have no standing independently of him, so too these elements are not found to stand either inside or outside each other, yet they have no standing independently of one another."[93] This explanation is justified on the following grounds: If they were to exist inside each other, then they would not perform their respective functions. If they were to exist outside each other, then they would be resolvable.[94] The principle of positional inseparability is also resorted to as a critique of the distinction between substance and quality. Hence it is contended that in the case of material elements which are positionally inseparable it is not possible to say: "This is the quality of that one and that is the quality of this one."[95]

The foregoing observations should show that the mental as well as the material *dhammas* are not actually separable one from another. In the case of the mental *dhammas*, the term used is *saṁsaṭṭha* (conjoined); in the case of the material *dhammas*, the term used is *avinibbhoga* (inseparable). This raises the question why the *dhammas* are presented as a plurality. The answer is that, although they are not actually separable, yet they are distinguishable (*vibhāgavanta*) one from another.[96] It is this distinguishability that serves as the foundation of the *dhamma* theory. Hence it is often mentioned in the Pāli sub-commentaries that the real nature of the things that are distinguishable can be brought into focus only through analysis.[97] This distinguishability is possible because although the *dhammas* are harmoniously blended (*ekato bhāvagata*), they are cognized severally (*gocaranānattatā*)[98] and are thus established as if they were separate entities. It is, however, maintained that material *dhammas* are much more easily distinguished than mental *dhammas*.[99] Thus, for instance, the distinction between colour, odour, taste, tactation, etc., is easy even for an ordinary person to make, while to distinguish mental phenomena one from another is said to be the most difficult task of all. This situation is well illustrated in the following reply given by Nāgasena Thera to King Milinda:

> "Suppose, O king, a man were to wade down into the sea, and taking some water in the palm of his hand, were to taste it with his tongue. Would he distinguish whether it were water from the Jumnā, or from the Aciravatī, or from the Mahī? More difficult than that, great king, is it to distinguish between the mental conditions which follow on the exercise of any one of the organs of sense, telling us that such is contact, and such sensation, and such idea, and such intention, and such thought."[100]

The other characteristic which was referred to earlier is the conditioned origination (*sappaccayatā*) of the *dhammas*. This is akin to the conception discussed above, for it also seeks to explain the nature of the *dhammas* from a synthetic point of view. In this connection five postulates are recognized as axiomatic, either implicitly or explicitly:

(i) It is not empirically possible to identify an absolute original cause of the "dhammic" process. Such a metaphysical conception is not in accord with Buddhism's empirical doctrine of causality, the purpose of which is not to explain how the world began but to describe the uninterrupted continuity of the saṁsāric process whose absolute beginning is not conceivable.[101] In this connection it must also be remembered that as a system of philosophy the Abhidhamma is descriptive and not speculative.

(ii) Nothing arises without the appropriate conditions necessary for its origination. This rules out the theory of fortuitous origination (*adhiccasamuppannavāda*).[102]

(iii) Nothing arises from a single cause. This rules out theories of a single cause (*ekakāraṇavāda*).[103] Their rejection is of great significance, showing that the Abhidhammic view of existence rejects all monistic theories which seek to explain the origin of the world from a single cause, whether this single cause is conceived as a personal God or an impersonal Godhead. It also serves as a critique of those metaphysical theories which attempt to reduce the world of experience to an underlying transempirical principle.

(iv) Nothing arises singly, as a solitary phenomenon.[104] Thus on the basis of a single cause or on the basis of a plurality of causes, a single effect does not arise. The invariable situation is that there is always a plurality of effects. It is on the rejection of the four views referred to above that the Abhidhammic doctrine of conditionality is founded.

(v) From a plurality of conditions a plurality of effects takes place. Applied to the *dhamma* theory, this means that a multiplicity of *dhammas* brings about a multiplicity of other *dhammas*.[105]

One implication that follows from the conditionality of the *dhammas* as discussed so far is that they invariably arise as clusters. This is true of both mental and material *dhammas*. Hence it is that whenever consciousness (*citta*) arises, together with it there arise at least seven mental concomitants (*cetasika*), namely, contact (*phassa*), sensation (*vedanā*), perception (*saññā*), volition (*cetanā*), one-pointedness (*ekaggatā*), psychic life (*arūpa-jīvitindriya*), and attention (*manasikāra*). These seven are called universal mental factors (*sabbacitta-sādhāraṇa*) because they are invariably present even in the most minimal unit of consciousness. Thus a psychic instance can never occur with less than eight constituents, i.e. consciousness and its seven invariable concomitants. Their relation is one of necessary conascence (*sahajāta*). We thus can see that even the smallest psychic unit or moment of consciousness turns out to be a complex correlational system. In the same way, the smallest unit of matter, which is called the basic octad (*suddhaṭṭhaka*), is in the ultimate analysis a cluster of (eight) material elements, namely, the four primary elements—earth, water, fire, and air—and four of the secondaries, colour, odour, taste, and nutritive essence (*ojā*). None of these eight material elements arises singly because they are necessarily conascent (*niyata-sahajāta*) and positionally inseparable (*padesato avinibbhoga*).[106] It will thus be seen that in the sphere of mind as well as in the domain of matter there are no solitary phenomena.

It is in the light of these observations that the question posed earlier as to whether the *dhammas* exhibit a unity or a plurality has to be discussed. The answer seems to veer towards both alternatives although it appears paradoxical to say so. In so far as the *dhammas* are distinguishable, one from another, to that extent they exhibit plurality. In so far as they are not actually separable, one from another, to that extent they exhibit unity. The reason for this situation is the methodological apparatus employed by the Ābhidhammikas in explaining the nature of empirical existence. As mentioned earlier, this consists of both analysis (*bheda*) and synthesis (*saṅgaha*). Analysis, when not supplemented by synthesis, leads to pluralism. Synthesis, when not supplemented by analysis, leads to monism. What one finds in the Abhidhamma is a *combined use* of both methods. This results in a philosophical vision which beautifully transcends the dialectical opposition between monism and pluralism.

III. Paññatti and the Two Truths

What emerges from this Abhidhammic doctrine of *dhammas* is a critical realism, one which (unlike idealism) recognizes the distinctness of the world from the experiencing subject yet also distinguishes between those types of entities that truly exist independently of the cognitive act and those that owe their being to the act of cognition itself. How does this doctrine interpret the "common-sense" view of the world, a kind of naive realism in the sense that it tends to recognize realities more or less corresponding to all linguistic terms? In other words, what relation is there between the *dhammas*, the ultimate elements of existence, and the objects of common-sense realism? What degree of reality, if any, could be bestowed on the latter?

It is in their answers to these questions that the Ābhidhammikas formulated the theory of *paññatti*—concepts or designations—together with a distinction drawn between two kinds of truth, conventional (*sammuti*) and absolute (*paramattha*). This theory assumes significance in another context. In most of the Indian philosophies which were associated with the *ātma*-tradition and subscribed to a substantialist view of existence, such categories as time and space came to be defined in absolute terms. The problem for the Ābhidhammikas was how to explain such categories without committing themselves to the same metaphysical assumptions. The theory of *paññatti* was the answer to this.

What may be described as the first formal definition of *paññatti* occurs in the *Dhammasaṅgaṇī*.[107] Here the three terms, *paññatti*, *nirutti,* and *adhivacana* are used synonymously and each term is defined by lumping together a number of appropriate equivalents. In Mrs. Rhys Davids' translation: "That which is an enumeration, that which is a designation, an expression (*paññatti*), a current term, a name, a denomination, the assigning of a name, an interpretation, a distinctive mark of discourse on this or that *dhamma*."[108] Immediately after this definition, a "predication of equipollent terms,"[109] it is observed that all the *dhammas* constitute the pathway of *paññattis* (*sabbe dhammā paññatti-pathā*).[110]

As shown by this definition, designation is the *paññatti*; what is designated thereby is the *paññatti-patha*. Whether the term *paññatti*, as used here, denotes the individual names given to each and every *dhamma* only, or whether it also denotes names assigned to various combinations of the *dhammas*, is not explicitly stated. According to the Abhidhamma, it may be noted, every combination of the objectively real *dhammas* represents a nominal reality, not an objective reality. The fact that the term *paññatti* includes names of both categories, the objective and the nominal, is suggested not only by what is stated elsewhere in the Abhidhamma Piṭaka,[111] but also by the later exegesis.[112] We may conclude then that according to the *Dhammasaṅgaṇī* definition, *paññatti* denotes all names, terms, and symbols that are expressive of the real existents as well as of their combinations in different forms.

Another important fact that should not be overlooked here is that according to the later exegesis *paññatti* includes not only names (*nāma*) but also ideas corresponding to them (*attha*).[113] Since the assignment of a designation creates an idea corresponding to it, we may interpret the above definition to include both. It is true, of course, that the *dhammas* do not exist in dependence on the operation of the mind, on their being designated by a term and conceptualized by mind. Nevertheless the assignment of names to the *dhammas* involves a process of conceptualization. Hence *paññatti* includes not only the names of things, whether they are real or nominal, but also all the concepts corresponding to them.

This theory of *paññatti*, presented as ancillary to the doctrine of *dhammas*, is not a complete innovation on the part of the Abhidhamma. Such a theory is clearly implied in the early Buddhist analysis of empirical existence into the aggregates, sense bases, and elements, and the only really new feature in the *paññatti* theory is its systematic formulation. Accordingly the term "person" becomes a common designation (*sammuti*) given to a congeries of dependently originated psycho-physical factors: "Just as there arises the name 'chariot' when there is a set of appropriate constituents, even so there comes to be this convention 'living being' when the five aggregates are present."[114] There is, however, this important difference to be noted: the early Buddhist idea of *sammuti* is not based on a formulated doctrine of real existents. Although what is analysed is called *sammuti*, that into which it is analysed is not called *paramattha*. Such a development is found only in the Abhidhamma, as we have already seen.

We should note that in the Abhidhamma, a clear distinction is drawn between *sammuti* and *paññātti*. *Paññatti*, as we have seen, refers to terms (*nāma*) expressive of things both real (*paramattha*) and convention-based (*sammuti*) and the ideas corresponding to them (*attha*). In contrast, *sammuti* is used in a restricted sense to mean only what is convention-based. It is this meaning that finds expression in the compound *sammuti-sacca* (conventional truth). That for the Abhidhamma *sammuti* is not the same as *paññatti* is also seen by the fact that in the *Dhammasaṅgaṇī* definition of *paññatti* quoted above, the term *sammuti* does not occur among its synonyms.

Although the theory of *paññatti* is formally introduced in the works of the Abhidhamma Piṭaka, it is in the Abhidhamma commentaries that we find more specific definitions of the term along with many explanations on the nature and scope of *paññattis* and on how they become objects of cognition. For example, because *paññattis* are without corresponding objective reality, the commentaries call them *asabhāva-dhammas*—things without a real nature—to distinguish them from the real elements of existence.[115] Since *sabhāva*, the intrinsic nature of a *dhamma*, is itself the *dhamma*, from the point of view of this definition what is qualified as *asabhāva* amounts to an *abhāva*, a non-existent in the final sense. It is in recognition of this fact that the three salient characteristics of empirical reality—origination (*uppāda*), subsistence (*ṭhiti*), and dissolution (*bhaṅga*)—are not applied to them. For these three characteristics can be predicated only of those things which answer to the Abhidhammic definition of empirical reality.[116] Again, unlike the real existents, *paññattis* are not brought about by conditions (*paccayaṭṭhitika*). For this same reason, they are also defined as "not positively produced" (*aparinipphanna*). Positive production (*parinipphannatā*) is true only of those things which have their own individual nature (*āveṇika-sabhāva*).[117] Only a *dhamma* that has an own-nature, with a beginning and an end in time, produced by conditions, and marked by the three salient characteristics of conditioned existence, is positively produced.[118]

Further, *paññattis* differ from *dhammas* in that only the latter are delimited by rise and fall; only of the *dhammas* and not of the *pannattis* can it be said, "They come into being having not been (*ahutvā sambhonti*); and, after having been, they cease (*hutvā paṭiventi*)."[119] *Paññattis* have no own-nature to be manifested in the three instants of arising, presence, and dissolution. Since they have no existence marked by these three phases, such temporal distinctions as past, present, and future do not apply to them. Consequently they have no reference to time (*kāla-vimutta*).[120] For this self-same reason, they have no place in the traditional analysis of empirical existence into the five *khandhas*, for what is included in the *khandhas* should have the characteristics of empirical reality and be subject to temporal divisions.[121]

Another noteworthy characteristic of *paññattis* is that they cannot be described either as conditioned (*saṅkhata*) or as unconditioned (*asaṅkhata*), for they do not possess their own-nature (*sabhāva*) to be so described.[122] Since the two categories of the conditioned and the unconditioned comprise all realities, the description of *paññattis* as exempt from these two categories is another way of underscoring their unreality.

What the foregoing observations amount to is that while a *dhamma* is a truly existent thing (*sabhāvasiddha*), a *paññatti* is a thing merely conceptualized (*parikappasiddha*).[123] The former is an existent verifiable by its own distinctive intrinsic characteristic,[124] but the latter, being a product of the mind's synthetic function, exists only by virtue of thought. It is a mental construct superimposed on things and hence possesses no objective counterpart. It is the imposition of oneness on what actually is a complex (*samūhekaggahaṇa*) that gives rise to *paññattis*.[125] With the dissolution of the appearance of unity (*ghaṇa-vinibbhoga*),[126] the oneness disappears and the complex nature is disclosed:

> Thus as when the component parts such as axles, wheels, frame, poles, etc., are arranged in a certain way, there comes to be the mere term of common usage "chariot," yet in the ultimate sense, when each part is examined, there is no chariot, and just as when the component parts of a house such as wattles, etc., are placed so that they enclose a space in a certain way, there comes to be the mere term of common usage "house," yet in the ultimate sense there is no house, and just as when trunk, branches, foliage, etc., are placed in a certain way, there comes to be the mere term of common usage "tree," yet in the ultimate sense, when each component is examined, there is no tree, so too, when there are the five aggregates (as objects) of clinging, there comes to be the mere term of common usage "a being," "a person," yet in the ultimate sense, when each component is examined, there is no being as a basis for the assumption "I am" or "I."[127]

In a similar way should be understood the imposition of oneness on what is complex.

Two kinds of *paññatti* are distinguished. One is called *nāma-paññatti* and the other *attha-paññatti*. The first refers to names, words, signs, or symbols through which things, real or unreal, are designated: "It is the mere mode of recognizing (*saññākāra-matta*) by way of this or that word whose significance is determined by worldly convention."[128] It is created by worldly consent (*lokasaṅketa-nimmitā*) and established by worldly usage (*lokavohārena siddhā*).[129] The other, called *attha-paññatti*, refers to ideas, notions, or concepts corresponding to the names, words, signs, or symbols. It is produced by the interpretative function of the mind (*kappanā*) and is based on the various forms or appearances presented by the real elements when they are in particular situations or positions (*avatthā-visesa*).[130] Both *nāma-paññatti* and *attha-paññatti* thus have a psychological origin and as such both are devoid of objective reality.

Nāma-paññatti is often defined as that which makes known (*paññāpanato paññatti*) and *attha-paññatti* as that which is made known (*paññāpiyattā paññatti*).[131] The former is an instance of agency definition (*kattu-sādhana*) and the latter of object definition (*kamma-sādhana*). What both attempt to show is that *nāma-paññatti* which makes *attha-paññatti* known, and *attha-paññatti* which is made known by *nāma-paññatti*, are mutually inter-dependent and therefore logically inseparable. This explains the significance of another definition which states that *nāma-paññatti* is the term's relationship with the ideas (*saddassa atthehi sambandho*) and that *attha-paññatti* is the idea's relationship with the terms (*atthassa saddehi sambandho*).[132] These two pairs of definition show that the two processes of conceptualization and verbalization through the symbolic medium of language are but two separate aspects of the same phenomenon. It is for the convenience of definition that what really amounts to a single phenomenon is treated from two different angles, which represent two ways of looking at the same thing.

The difference is established by defining the same word, *paññatti*, in two different ways. When it is defined as subject it is *nāma-paññatti*—the concept as name. When it is defined as object it is *attha-paññatti*—the concept as meaning. If the former is that which expresses (*vācaka*), the latter is that which is expressible (*vacanīya*).[133] In this same sense, if the former is *abhidhāna*, the latter is *abhidheya*.[134] Since *attha-paññatti* stands for the process of conceptualization it represents more the subjective and dynamic aspect, and since *nāma-paññatti* stands for the process of verbalization it represents more the objective and static aspect. For the assignment of a term to what is constructed in thought—in other words, its expression through the symbolic medium of language—invests it with some kind of relative permanence and objectivity. It is, so to say, crystallized into an entity.

Now the definition of *attha-paññatti* as that which is made known by *nāma-paññatti* gives rise to the question as to what its position is in relation to the real existents (*dhammas*). For if the real existents, too, can be made known (= *attha-paññatti*), on what basis are the two categories, the real and conceptual, to be distinguished? What should not be overlooked here is that according to its very definition *attha-paññatti* exists by virtue of its being conceived (*parikappiyamāna*) and expressed (*paññāpiyamāna*). Hence it is incorrect to explain *attha-paññatti* as that which is conceptualizable and expressible, for its very existence stems from the act of being conceptualized and expressed. This rules out the possibility of its existing without being conceptualized and expressed. In the case of the *dhammas* or real existents the situation is quite different. While they can be made known by *nāma-paññatti*, their existence is not dependent on their being known or conceptualized. Where such a real existent is made known by a *nāma-paññatti*, the latter is called *vijjamāna-paññatti*,[135] because it represents something that exists in the real and ultimate sense (*paramatthato*). And the notion or concept (= *attha-paññatti*) corresponding to it is called *tajjā-paññatti*, the verisimilar or appropriate concept.[136] This does not mean that the real existent has transformed itself into a concept. It only means that a concept corresponding to it has been established.

If the doctrine of *dhammas* led to its ancillary theory of *paññatti* as discussed above, both in turn led to another development, i.e. the distinction drawn between two kinds of truth as *sammuti-sacca* (conventional truth) and *paramattha-sacca* (absolute truth). Although this distinction is an Abhidhammic innovation it is not completely dissociated from the early Buddhist teachings. For the antecedent trends that led to its formulation can be traced to the early Buddhist scriptures themselves. One such instance is the distinction drawn in the Aṅguttara Nikāya between *nītattha* and *neyyattha*.[137] The former refers to those statements which have their meaning "drawn out" (*nīta-attha*), i.e. to be taken as they stand, as explicit and definitive statements. The latter refers to those statements which require their meaning "to be drawn out" (*neyya-attha*). The distinction alluded to here may be understood in a broad way to mean the difference between the direct and the indirect meaning.

The distinction is so important that to overlook it is to misrepresent the teachings of the Buddha: "Whoever declares a discourse with a meaning already drawn out as a discourse with a meaning to be drawn out and (conversely) whoever declares a discourse with a meaning to be drawn out as a discourse with a meaning already drawn out, such a one makes a false statement with regard to the Blessed One."[138] It seems very likely that this distinction between *nītattha* and *neyyattha* has provided a basis for the emergence of the subsequent doctrine of double truth. In point of fact, the commentary to the Aṅguttara Nikāya seeks to establish a correspondence between the original sutta-passage and the Theravāda version of the two kinds of truth.[139]

One interesting feature in the Theravāda version of the theory is the use of the term *sammuti* for relative truth. For in all other schools of Buddhist thought the term used is *saṁvṛti*. The difference is not simply that between Pāli and Sanskrit, for the two terms differ both in etymology and meaning. The term *sammuti* is derived from the root *man*, to think, and when prefixed with *sam* it means consent, convention, general agreement. On the other hand, the term *saṁvṛti* is derived from the root *vṛ*, to cover, and when prefixed with *sam* it means covering, concealment. This difference is not confined to the vocabulary of the theory of double truth alone. That elsewhere, too, Sanskrit *saṁvṛti* corresponds to Pāli *sammuti* is confirmed by other textual instances.[140] Since *sammuti* refers to convention or general agreement, *sammuti-sacca* means truth based on convention or general agreement. On the other hand, the idea behind *saṁvṛti-satya* is that which covers up the true nature of things and makes them appear otherwise.[141]

The validity of the two kinds of statement corresponding to *sammuti* and *paramattha* is set out as follows:

> Statements referring to convention-based things (*saṅketa*) are valid because they are based on common agreement; statements referring to ultimate categories (*paramattha*) are valid because they are based on the true nature of the real existents.[142]

As shown here, the distinction between the two truths depends on the distinction between *saṅketa* and *paramattha*. Now, *saṅketa* includes things which depend for their being on mental interpretations superimposed on the category of the real.[143] For instance, the validity of the term "table" is based, not on an objective existent corresponding to the term, but on mental interpretation superimposed on a congeries of material *dhammas* organized in a particular manner. Although a table is not a separate reality distinct from the material *dhammas* that enter into its composition, nevertheless the table is said to exist because in common parlance it is accepted as a separate reality. On the other hand, the term *paramattha* denotes the category of real existents (*dhammas*) which have their own objective nature (*sabhāva*). Their difference may be set out as follows: When a particular situation is explained on the basis of terms indicative of the real elements of existence (the *dhammas*), that explanation is *paramattha-sacca*. When the self-same situation is explained on the basis of terms indicative of things which have their being dependent on the mind's synthetic function (i.e. *paññatti*), that explanation is *sammuti-sacca*. The validity of the former is based on its correspondence to the ultimate data of empirical reality. The validity of the latter is based on its correspondence to things established by conventions.

As pointed out by K.N. Jayatilleke in his *Early Buddhist Theory of Knowledge*, one misconception about the Theravāda version of double truth is that *paramattha-sacca* is superior to *sammuti-sacca* and that "what is true in the one sense is false in the other."[144] This observation that the distinction in question is not based on a theory of degrees of truth will become clear from the following free translation of the relevant passages contained in three commentaries:

> Herein references to living beings, gods, Brahmā, etc., are *sammuti-kathā*, whereas references to impermanence, suffering, egolessness, the aggregates of the empiric individuality, the spheres and elements of sense perception and mind-cognition, bases of mindfulness, right effort, etc., are *paramattha-kathā*. One who is capable of understanding and penetrating to the truth and hoisting the flag of arahantship when the teaching is set out in terms of generally accepted conventions, to him the Buddha preaches the doctrine based on *sammuti-kathā*. One who is capable of understanding and penetrating to the truth and hoisting the flag of arahantship when the teaching is set out in terms of ultimate categories, to him the Buddha preaches the doctrine based on *paramattha-kathā*. To one who is capable of awakening to the truth through *sammuti-kathā*, the teaching is not presented on the basis of *paramattha-kathā*, and conversely, to one who is capable of awakening to the truth through *paramattha-kathā*, the teaching is not presented on the basis of *sammuti-kathā*.
>
> There is this simile on this matter. Just as a teacher of the three Vedas who is capable of explaining their meaning in different dialects might teach his pupils, adopting the particular dialect which each pupil understands, even so the Buddha preaches the doctrine adopting, according to the suitability of the occasion, either the *sammuti-* or the *paramattha-kathā*. It is by taking into consideration the ability of each individual to understand the Four Noble Truths that the Buddha presents his teaching either by way of *sammuti* or by way of *paramattha* or by way of both. Whatever the method adopted the purpose is the same, to show the way to Immortality through the analysis of mental and physical phenomena.[145]

As shown from the above quotation, the penetration of the truth is possible by either teaching, the conventional or the ultimate, or by the combination of both. One method is not singled out as superior or inferior to the other. It is like using the dialect that a person readily understands, and there is no implication that one dialect is either superior or inferior to another. What is more, as the commentary to the Aṅguttara Nikāya states specifically, whether the Buddhas preach the doctrine according to *sammuti* or *paramattha*, they teach only what is true, only what accords with actuality, without involving themselves in what is not true (*amusā'va*).[146] The statement: "The person exists" (= *sammuti-sacca*) is not erroneous, provided one does not imagine by the person a substance enduring in time. Convention requires the use of such terms, but as long as one does not imagine substantial entities corresponding to them, such statements are valid.[147] On the other hand, as the commentators observe, if for the sake of conforming to the ultimate truth one would say, "The five aggregates eat" (*khandhā bhuñjanti*), "The five aggregates walk" (*khandhā gacchanti*), instead of saying: "A person eats," "A person walks," such a situation would result in what is called *vohārabheda*, i.e. a breach of convention resulting in a breakdown in meaningful communication.[148]

Hence in presenting the teaching the Buddha does not exceed linguistic conventions (*na hi Bhagavā samaññaṁ atidhāvati*),[149] but uses such terms as "person" without being led astray by their superficial implications (*aparāmasaṁ voharati*).[150] Because the Buddha is able to employ such linguistic designations as "person" and "individual" without assuming corresponding substantial entities, he is called "skilled in expression" (*vohāra-kusala*).[151] The use of such terms does not in any way involve falsehood.[152] Skilfulness in the use of words is the ability to conform to conventions (*sammuti*), usages (*vohāra*), designations (*paññatti*), and turns of speech (*nirutti*) in common use in the world without being led astray by them.[153] Hence in understanding the teaching of the Buddha one is advised not to adhere dogmatically to the mere superficial meanings of words.[154]

The foregoing observations should show that according to the Theravāda version of double truth, one kind of truth is not held to be superior to the other. Another interesting conclusion to which the foregoing observations lead is that as far as the Theravāda is concerned, the distinction between *sammuti-sacca* and *paramattha-sacca* does not refer to two kinds of truth as such but to two ways of presenting the truth. Although they are formally introduced as two kinds of truth, they are explained as two modes of expressing what is true. They do not represent two degrees of truth of which one is superior or inferior to the other. This explains why the two terms, *kathā* (speech) and *desanā* (discourse), are often used with reference to the two kinds of truth.[155] In this respect the distinction between *sammuti* and *paramattha* corresponds to the distinction made in the earlier scriptures between *nītattha* and *neyyattha*. For, as we saw earlier, no preferential value-judgement is made between *nītattha* and *neyyattha*. All that is emphasized is that the two kinds of statement should not be confused. The great advantage in presenting *sammuti* and *paramattha* in this way is that it does not raise the problem of reconciling the concept of a plurality of truths with the well-known statement of the Suttanipāta: "Truth is indeed one, there is no second" (*ekaṁ hi saccaṁ na dutīyam atthi*).[156]

Notes

1. The term *dhamma* denotes not only the ultimate data of empirical existence but also the unconditioned state of Nibbāna. In this study, however, only the former aspect is taken into consideration.
2. The reference here is to its general sense. In its special sense *nāma-rūpa* means the following psycho-physical aspects: "Sensation, perception, will, contact, attention—this is called *nāma*. The four material elements and the form depending on them—this is called *rūpa*" (S II 3). In the oft-recurrent statement, *viññāṇapaccayā nāmarūpaṁ*, the reference is to the special sense.
3. See e.g. S III 47, 86-87; M III 16.
4. See e.g. S II 248; III 231.
5. See e.g. D II 302; III 102, 243; A III 400; V 52.
6. See e.g. S II 140; D I 79; III 38; A I 255; III 17.
7. S III 49.
8. Cf. *Aññatra paccayā natthi viññāṇassa sambhavo* (M III 281).
9. See Dhs. 5ff.
10. Nyanaponika Thera, *Abhidhamma Studies* (Kandy, 1976), p.21.
11. Cf. *The Central Conception of Buddhism* (London, 1923); *Buddhist Logic* (reprint: New York, 1962), Vol. I, Introduction.
12. Nyanaponika Thera, p.41.
13. VsmṬ 137.
14. S II 17, 77.
15. Ibid.
16. S II 77.
17. Ibid.
18. For a short but lucid description, see Nārada Thera, *A Manual of Abhidhamma* (Colombo, 1957), Vol. II, pp.87ff.
19. See "L'origine des sectes bouddhiques d'apres Paramārtha," trans. P. Demievielle, *Mélanges Chinois et Bouddhiques*, Vol. I, 1932, pp.57ff.; J. Masuda, "Origin and Doctrines of Early Indian Buddhist Schools" (trans. of Vasumitra's Treatise), *Asia Major*, Vol. II, 1925, pp.53–57; Edward Conze, *Buddhist Thought in India* (London, 1962), pp.122ff.; A.K. Warder, *Indian Buddhism* (Delhi, 1970), pp.289ff.

20. Kvu 1ff. See too the relevant sections of its commentary.

21. Ibid.

22. Cf. *Ahutvā sambhūtaṁ hutvā na bhavissati* (Psm 76). *Evaṁ sabbe pi rūpārūpino dhammā ahutvā sambhonti hutvā paṭiventi* (Vsm 512).

23. See Y. Karunadasa, "Vibhajyavāda versus Sarvāstivāda: The Buddhist Controversy on Time," *Kalyani: Journal of Humanities and Social Sciences* (Colombo, 1983), Vol.II, pp.16ff.

24. Cf. e.g. MhNdA 261; DhsA 126; VsmS V 6.

25. See ADSVṬ 4. Cf. *Cintetī ti cittaṁ. Ārammaṇaṁ vijānātī ti attho. Yathāha: Visayavijānanalakkhaṇaṁ cittan ti. Sati hi nissayasamanantarādipaccaye na vinā ārammaṇena cittaṁ uppajjatī ti tassa tā lakkhaṇatā vuttā. Etena nirālambanavādīmataṁ paṭikkhittaṁ hoti* (ibid.).

26. Ibid.

27. Ibid.

28. *Na nippariyāyato labbhati* (ibid.). Cf. *Svāyaṁ kattuniddeso pariyāyaladdho, dhammato aññassa kattunivattanattho.* VismṬ 141.

29. Cf. *Paramatthato ekasabhāvopi sabhāvadhammo pariyāyavacanehi viya samāropitarūpehi bahūhi pakārehi pakāsīyati. Evaṁ hi so suṭṭhu pakāsito hotī ti* (Abhvk 117). *Sakasaka-kiccesu hi dhammānaṁ attappadhānatāsamāropanena kattubhāvo, tadanukūlabhāvena taṁsampayutte dhammasamūhe kattubhāvasamāropanena (paṭipādetabbassa) dhammassa karaṇatthañ ca pariyāyato labbhati* (ibid. 16).

30. VsmṬ 484.

31. Ibid. 491.

32. DṬ 28.

33. *Cittacetasikānaṁ dhammānaṁ bhāvasādhanam eva nippariyāyato labbhati.* Abhvk 16; ADSVṬ 4.

34. *Na ca sabhāvā añño dhammo nāma atthi* (AMṬ 21).

35. *Dhammamatta-dīpanaṁ sabhāva-padaṁ* (ibid. 70).

36. *Sabhāvavinimmuttā kāci kiriyā nāma natthi* (Abhvk 210).

37. *Dhammo ti sabhāvo.* (AMṬ 121).

38. *Bodheyyajanānurodhavasena* (DṬ 76).

39. *Dhammato añño kattā natthī ti dassetuṁ* (ibid. 673). Cf. *Dhammato*

aññassa kattunivattanatthaṁ dhammam eva kattāraṁ niddisati (AMṬ 66); see also VsmS V 184, VsmṬ 484.

40. Vsm 513.

41. *Nāmarūpato uddhaṁ issarādīnaṁ abhāvato* (ibid.).

42. VsmṬ 482.

43. Abhvk 393.

44. VsmṬ 482.

45. Abhvk 123.

46. Psm II 211.

47. Abhvk 414; DhsA 63; PsmA 18; Mvn 6.

48. *Na ca dhāriyamāna-sabhāvā añño dhammo nāma atthi* (AMṬ 21). *Na hi ruppanādīhi aññe rūpādayo kakkhaḷādīhi ca aññe paṭhavī-ādayo dhammā vijjantī ti. Aññathā pana avabodhetuṁ na sakkā ti ... sabhāvadhamme aññe viya katvā attano sabhāvaṁ dhārentī ti vuttaṁ* (ibid. 22).

49. *Yathāpaccayaṁ hi pavattimattaṁ etaṁ sabhāvadhammo* (VsmT 462). See also Abhvk 116; VsmS V 132.

50. *Attano eva vā bhāvo etasmiṁ natthī ti sabhāvena suññaṁ* (PsmA III 634).

51. *Attano lakkhaṇam dhārentī ti dhammā* (VbhA 45). See also VsmS V 273; VsmṬ 359.

52. PsmA I 16; VsmṬ 24.

53. SA II 213; Vsm 520.

54. *Abhede pi bheda-parikappanā* (Abhvk 156).

55. VsmṬ 362.

56. ADSVṬ 32; ADSS 52.

57. Vsm 321.

58. Cf. *Nanu ca kakkhaḷattam eva paṭhavīdhātū ti? Saccam etaṁ. Tathā pi ... abhinne pi dhamme kappanāsiddhena bhedena evaṁ niddeso kato. Evaṁ hi atthavisesāvabodho hoti* (VsmṬ 362).

59. DṬ 105. Cf. *Rūpakkhandhass'eva hi etaṁ (ruppanalakkhaṇaṁ), na vedanādīnaṁ. Tasmā paccattalakkhaṇan ti vuccati. Aniccadukkh-ānattalakkhaṇaṁ pana vedanādīnam pi hoti. Tasmā taṁ sāmañña-lakkhaṇan ti vuccati* (SA II 291).

60. See ADSVṬ 32.

61. These are the three phases of a momentary *dhamma*, according to the Theravāda version of the theory of moments.

62. See Abhvk 288; Mvn 67.

63. *Na hi jāti jāyati jarā jīrati maraṇaṁ mīyatī ti voharituṁ yuttaṁ, anavaṭṭhānato* (Mvn 67–68).

64. DṬ 105.

65. ADSVṬ 4.

66. ADSS 3.

67. Mvn 258.

68. Ibid.; Abhvk 123.

69. Mvn 258; KvuA 8.

70. *Attano pana bhūtatāya eva saccikaṭṭho* (Mvn 259).

71. Bhikkhu Ñāṇamoli, *The Path of Purification* (Colombo, 1956), p.421.

72. Vsm II 159.

73. See VsmṬ 227; Mvn 258; ItiA 142.

74. Abhvk 445.

75. Cf. *Saṅkhatāsaṅkhatapaññattidhammesu na koci dhammo ārammaṇapaccayo na hotī ti dasseti. Ten'eva hi "yaṁ yaṁ dhammaṁ ārabbhā" ti aniyamo kato ti. Nanu ca "yaṁ yaṁ dhamman" ti vuttattā paññattiyā gahaṇaṁ na hotī ti? Nāyaṁ doso. Dhammasaddassa ñeyyavācakattā* (Abhv 445).

76. Abhvk 346. Cf. *Na hi abhāvassa koci sabhāvo atthi* (VsmṬ 539).

77. Abhvk 4; VsmṬ 225: *salakkhaṇa-saṅkhāto aviparīta-sabhāvo.*

78. *Lakkhaṇa-anaññathatta* (ADSVṬ 62).

79. *Na hi sabhāvā kenaci sahabhāvena saṁ sabhāvaṁ jahanti* (Mvn 69).

80. *Na hi kālabhedena dhammānaṁ sabhāvabhedo atthi* (VsmṬ 197; ADSVṬ 123).

81. Vsm 376, 381; AMṬ 43; Tkp 59.

82. Tkp 62ff.

83. *Na ca labbhā imesaṁ dhammānaṁ vinibbhujitvā vinibbhujitvā nānākaraṇaṁ paññāpetuṁ* (M I 480).

84. Mil 58–59.

85. *The Questions of King Milinda*, trans. T.W. Rhys Davids (reprint: New York, 1963), p.97.
86. For other illustrations, see DhsA 273, MA II 287, Abhvk 293.
87. DhsA 270.
88. See ADS 28; VsmS 389.
89. See VsmṬ 451; Abhvk 273.
90. See Tkp 3, 14, 16; ADS 28.
91. VsmṬ 451; Abhvk 273.
92. See Y. Karunadasa, *Buddhist Analysis of Matter* (Colombo, 1967), p.26.
93. Vsm 387.
94. VsmṬ 364; see also Abhvk 248.
95. Vsm 444–45.
96. See e.g. ADSVṬ 5; VsmṬ 21; Abhvk 22.
97. *Vibhāgavantānaṁ dhammānaṁ sabhāvavibhāvanaṁ vibhāgena eva hoti* (Abhvk 22; VsmṬ 470).
98. Mil 58–59.
99. MA II 287.
100. *Questions of King Milinda*, p.142.
101. *Anamataggo'yaṁ bhikkhave saṁsāro; pubbā koṭi na paññāyati* (S II 178).
102. D I 28; Ud 69.
103. DhsA 78.
104. *Ekassa dhammassa uppatti paṭisedhito hoti* (ibid. 79).
105. Ibid. 78ff.
106. See *A Manual of Abhidhamma* (trans. of ADS), Nārada Thera (Colombo, 1956), pp.79ff.; Karunadasa, *Buddhist Analysis of Matter*, pp.155ff.
107. *Yā tesaṁ tesaṁ dhammānaṁ saṅkhā samaññā paññatti vohāro nāmaṁ nāmakammaṁ nāmadheyyaṁ nirutti vyañjanaṁ abhilāpo* (Dhs 110).
108. *Buddhist Manual of Psychological Ethics* (trans. of Dhs), C.A.F. Rhys-Davids (London, 1923), p.340.
109. Ibid.

110. Dhs 110.
111. Cf. Kvu controversy on the concept of person (*puggala*).
112. See below, p. 35.
113. See below, pp. 33-34.
114. S I 135.
115. Abhvk 346.
116. See KvuA 198–99.
117. AMṬ 114ff.
118. Ibid. 116.
119. VsmṬ 210.
120. Cf. *Vināsabhāvato atītādikālavasena na vattabbattā nibbānaṁ paññatti ca kālavimuttā nāma* (ADSVṬ 36).
121. MA II 299.
122. Cf. *Saṅkhatāsaṅkhatalakkhaṇānaṁ pana abhāvena na vattabbā saṅkhatā ti vā asaṅkhatā ti vā* (KvuA 92).
123. ADSVṬ 52–53.
124. *Aññamaññabyatirekena paramatthato upalabbhati* (VsmṬ 198).
125. Ibid. 137.
126. DṬ 123.
127. Ñāṇamoli, *Path of Purification*, p.458.
128. VsmṬ 225.
129. ADSVṬ 53.
130. ADSVṬ 151; Abhvk 317ff.; MilṬ 7–8.
131. ADS 39; ADSVṬ 151; SS vv.37ff.; PV v.1066.
132. ADSSV 53.
133. ADSS 159.
134. ADSSV 54.
135. SS v.68; MA I 55.
136. Ibid.
137. A II 60.
138. Ibid.
139. AA II 118.
140. See e.g. *Bodhisattvabhūmi*, ed. U. Wogihara (Tokyo, 1930–36), p.48.

Perhaps the only single Theravāda text where *saṁvṛti* is used instead of the usual *sammuti* is the Sinhala *sanné* to ADS; see ADSS 159.

141. See *Bodhicaryāvatāra-pañjikā* (Bibliotheca Indica, Calcutta, 1904–14), p.170. For a detailed account of the theories of truth as presented by various Buddhist schools, see L. de la Vallée Poussin, "Les Deux, Les Quatre, Les Trois Verités," *Mélanges chinois et bouddhiques*, Vol. V, pp.159ff.

142. *Saṅketavacanaṁ saccaṁ lokasammutikāraṇā*
Paramatthavacanaṁ saccaṁ dhammānaṁ bhūtalakkhaṇā.
(AA I 54; KvuA 34; DA I 251)

143. See SS vv.3ff.

144. Jayatilleke, p.364.

145. AA I 54–55; DA I 251–52; SA II 77.

146. DA I 251.

147. See Jayatilleke, p.365.

148. SA I 51.

149. KvuA 103.

150. Cf. KvuA 103: *Atthi puggalo ti vacana-mattato abhiniveso na kātabbo.*

151. SA I 51.

152. Cf. MA 125:

Tasmāvohāra-kusalassa lokanāthassa satthuno
Sammutiṁ voharantassa musāvādo na jāyati.

153. DA I 251.

154. *Na vacanabhedamattaṁ ālambitabbaṁ* (Abhvt 88).

155. AA I 54; Abhvk 324.

156. Suttanipāta v.884.

Abbreviations

A	Aṅguttaranikāya
AA	Aṅguttaranikāya Aṭṭhakathā
Abhvk	Abhidhammatthavikāsinī, ed. A.P. Buddhadatta (Colombo, 1961)
Abhvt	Abhidhammāvatāra
ADS	Abhidhammatthasaṅgaha
ADSS	Abhidharmārthasaṁgraha-sannaya; included in Abhidhammatthasaṅgaha, ed. by Paññāmoli Tissa (Ambalangoda, 1926)
ADSSV	Abhidhammatthasaṅgaha-Saṅkhepavaṇṇanā, ed. W. Paññānanda Thera (Colombo, 1899)
ADSVṬ	Abhidhammatthasaṅgaha-Vibhāvinī-Ṭīkā, ed. D. Paññānanda (Colombo, 1899)
AMṬ	Abhidhamma-Mūlaṭīkā, ed. D. Paññāsāra and P. Vimaladhamma (Colombo, 1939)
D	Dīghanikāya
DA	Dīghanikāya Aṭṭhakathā
Dhs	Dhammasaṅgaṇī
DhsA	Dhammasaṅgaṇī Aṭṭhakathā
DṬ	Dīghanikāya-Ṭīkā (Colombo, 1974)
ItiA	Itivuttaka Aṭṭhakathā
Kvu	Kathāvatthu
KvuA	Kathāvatthu Aṭṭhakathā
M	Majjhimanikāya
MA	Majjhimanikāya Aṭṭhakathā
MhNdA	Mahāniddesa Aṭṭhakathā
Mil	Milindapañha
MilṬ	Milinda Ṭīkā

Mvn	Mohavicchedanī
Psm	Paṭisambhidāmagga
PsmA	Paṭisambhidāmagga Aṭṭhakathā
Pv	Paramatthavinicchaya
S	Saṁyuttanikāya
SA	Saṁyuttanikāya Aṭṭhakathā
SS	Saccasaṅkhepa (PTS Journal, 1917-19)
Tkp	Tikapaṭṭhāna
Ud	Udāna
Vbh	Vibhaṅga
VbhA	Vibhaṅga Aṭṭhakathā
Vsm	Visuddhimagga
VsmS	Visuddhimārgasannaya, ed. M. Dharmaratna (Colombo, 1890-1917)
VsmṬ	Visuddhimagga Ṭīkā (Paramatthamañjūsā), ed. M. Dhammananda (Colombo, 1928)

All references are to PTS eds. unless indicated otherwise.

Of related interest

A Comprehensive Manual of Abhidhamma

Edited by Bhikkhu Bodhi

The Abhidhamma is the Buddhist analysis of mind and mental processes, a wide-ranging systematization of the Buddha's teaching that combines philosophy, psychology, and ethics into a unique and remarkable synthesis. For over 800 years a little treatise called the Abhidhammattha Sangaha has served as the key to open this treasure store of Buddhist wisdom. The present volume offers an exact translation of the Sangaha along with a detailed explanatory guide designed to lead the reader through the complexities of this ancient "psychology of liberation." The book specially features 48 charts and tables which represent the subject in a visually accessible format.

Hardback 432 pages BP 304H

Of related interest

The Visuddhimagga
The Path of Purification

Translated by Bhikkhu Ñāṇamoli

The *Visuddhimagga* is the "great treatise" of Theravada Buddhism, an encyclopedic manual of Buddhist doctrine and meditation written in the fifth centuy by the great Buddhist commentator, Ācariya Buddhaghosa. The treatise aims at organizing the various teachings of the Buddha found in the Pāli Canon into a clear and comprehensive map of the path leading to the final Buddhist goal. In the course of his work Buddhaghosa gives detailed instructions on the forty subjects of serenity meditation; an elaborate account of the Abhidhamma philosophy; and detailed descriptions of the stages of insight culminating in final liberation. The translation by Bhikkhu Ñāṇamoli ranks as an outstanding cultural achievement.

Hardback   950 pages   BP 207H

THE BUDDHIST PUBLICATION SOCIETY

The BPS is an approved charity dedicated to making known the Teaching of the Buddha, which has a vital message for people of all creeds. Founded in 1958, the BPS has published a wide variety of books and booklets covering a great range of topics. Its publications include accurate annotated translations of the Buddha's discourses, standard reference works, as well as original contemporary expositions of Buddhist thought and practice. These works present Buddhism as it truly is—a dynamic force which has influenced receptive minds for the past 2500 years and is still as relevant today as it was when it first arose. A full list of our publications will be sent upon request. Write to:

The Hony. Secretary
BUDDHIST PUBLICATION SOCIETY
P.O. Box 61
54, Sangharaja Mawatha
Kandy • Sri Lanka